1950

D0999742

NEAR AND FAR

By the same Author

POETRY

The Shepherd

English Poems

Retreat

PROSE

The Bonadventure

On the Poems of Henry Vaughan

Leigh Hunt's "Examiner" Examined
(with newly discovered papers by Charles Lamb)

Undertones of War

EDITIONS

John Clare: Poems chiefly from MS. (with Alan Porter)

A Song to David, with other Poems by Christopher Smart

NEAR AND FAR

New Poems by

EDMUND BLUNDEN

Harper & Brothers Publishers
New York and London
1930

C-E

PRINTED IN THE UNITED STATES

Dedicated to that honest friend and admired poet,
William Force Stead ❧

PREFATORY NOTE

These poems are chiefly the product of the last two years. The Japanese pieces, however, are mainly reprinted from a volume issued by Mr. C. W. Beaumont in 1927 in a limited and decorated edition. For the previous appearance of several items I am indebted to the editors of the "Observer," "London Mercury," "Nation," "Fortnightly," "English Review," "Daily Express," "New Statesman," and "Saturday Review."

It is not my habit to reply to my critics, who have been generous to me as a versifier for years. But, in respect of the Japanese pieces which I have written–and I hope to write more–I may be allowed a word. They were blamed here and there for their English tone, and their author was described as an incorrigible "Briton." Those, however, who go from England to Japan without succumbing first to Japanesery will find that there is no great gulf between the old experiences and the new. Substitute cherry-blossom for rose, and rice for bread, and Alps for Chilterns–you do not thereby produce a mystical incomprehensibility. That is better (and worse) provided by avoiding Japan and the Japanese and just being "Oriental."

E. B.

CONTENTS

THE GEOGRAPHER'S GLORY
or, The Globe in 1730

THE GEOGRAPHER'S GLORY

or, The Globe in 1730

When through the windows buzzed the way-
lost bee
Into a drowsy room that held no honey,
Whose solemn clock surveyed the merry swarm
Of boys intent on chapbook and fools' tricks,
At length the old Geographer resumed
His desk; when several close observers noted
Signs that his late reappearance might be due
To a well-met friend, and the cheerful bottle to
give him.
Meanwhile the master, laying down his hat,
His gold-laced hat, and tossing his wig's three tails,
Poising a quill, and letting it fall to the floor,
Replacing his hat, caressing a small Globe,
Saddling his nose, descanted thus:
"Boys, boys,
I must desire you'll ever pay respect
To our most ripe, most profitable theme,
The Globe, and grammar of Geography.
It is a mine, exceeding rich Peru,
And, though some owlish critics dub it dry,

Exceeds for banquet-like variety
The City feast. Observe this Globe. My lads,
The vast terraqueous ball whereon we dwell,
And here with newest nicety represented,
Is full of wonders, which our countrymen
And others of congenial quality
Have with much circumstance of truth reported.
—Away, ye flies; back to Beelzebub.—
I, yes, as I was saying, this grand Globe
Is full of wonders. While the pallid herd
Of Graecians limit their pedantic gaze
To some prodigious "nominativius pendens,"
Or harry some Athenian cobbler's ghost,
Let us imbibe—I say, let us imbibe
Full draughts from our true Arethusan fountains.

As I, this very moment, sit in London
(And do not know where I could sit more gladly)
I scan the extended masterpiece of Earth:
By this Globe's use we readily determine
The hour when the Great Mogul sits to dine
In India, or the Czar in Muscovy.
This Globe assures me, there's a place on Earth
Where, though the air blows pure, the "genius loci"

Is such that no two friends can there continue
In mutual love and friendship for two minutes.
O sad amazement, should two noble youths
(Collins for instance and—you, you rascal
Hargrave)
Of virtue and of studious parts, who long
Shared the same attic, pored on the same map,
Be shipwrecked there!
Now in the South of China,
A certain city's numerous population
Both male and female, though they use the gait
That commonly is used in Paul's Church-Yard,
Appear to strangers walking on their heads,
Inverted. O, but one of many marvels.
Blest be the Globe! O that the Lord would grant me
Before I die a journey into Denmark,
There to survey the famous Globes in Gottorp,
And honour Tycho Brahe. But less cheerly
Would I in New Castile draw near that Lake
Which in presentiment of hurricanoes
Raves at the sky, and howls man on to doom.

These truths surpass all fiction; yet truth bids
I should not daub where she herself is plain.

You have heard high legends of the Elysian Fields,
The poet's vaunted theme; but, in the fact,
They are an ordinary plot of ground,
Where higglers tie the goat or panniered ass,
Near Naples.

I must, in parenthesis,
Observe, that the opening mind's credulity
Stands in much danger from these plaguy poets.
Avoid their siren song, boys; learn betimes
To shun the glittering counterfeit of rhymes.
Thus freed the maze of error, forth we rove
On our grand tour of reason and delight;
Whether to pause among the holy relics
Of Palestine, and view the cave and fountain
Whence great St. John emerged with burning eye
To make the greater Prophet's pathway plain,
Or find each several scene of that high Suffering
By which we hope at length to inhabit heaven.
Truth still shall guide us; even at Scanderoon,
Though Jonah's Pillar be alleged the place
Where the vast Fish disgorged the man of grief,
We must reserve some doubt. Yet, did we yield
Entire persuasion there, our fault were less
Than what some dreaming ancients make, who'd hold

The Whale swam round one quarter of the World
Within three sunsets.
O most crude Excess,
Base Non-Geography, ye weeds of life,
And obstinate as Jews, who would not hear
The Joyful Gospel first announced to them
By Christ with musical appeal, heard not,
Saw not, and keep their stiff necks to this day.

Still as we go, the teeming mind of Heaven
Supplies each query, and wonder walks with use:
Our trees, in temperate Britain, that embower
Noble estates, and cool the alehouse bench,
Become those wooden walls that Spain respects,
And leafy rustling grows the Lion's roaring.
To several regions, several trees; there's one
In Mexico, where shops are few, that gives
Honey and vinegar, water, oil and wine—
Its limpid liquor passes as all these
By shrewd contrivance. Mark as well, my lads,
That on Molucca coast, where the burnt air
Proposes to sea-captains strong desire
For stronger liquor, there the moral Clove
Abounds, rich cargo; virtuous to absorb

Whatever wine it neighbours. Whence it chances
That often some bold boatswain, fondly drawn
Towards the insidious hogshead, bawling hymns,
Stops, stares, starts, rages at the emptied store,
And sees too late the bags of Cloves beside.
Him I may liken to the Java tree
That, at the rising of the sun, lets fall
Its midnight buds, and in the heat all day
Stands melancholy in a funeral robe.

But time contracts my amphitheatre,
Time, that consumed even Nineveh, the maw
To which even this our City is a morsel.
I know no monster in the world like him
For hunger, wildness and sad speech; not one.
And yet there dwells in Ethiopian pools
A creature with a sighing dolorous tone
Of which report is full; the sweetest sorrow
Fills the air there, beyond Amara's mountain,
And Nubia with her poisons; those, alas,
May be the sources of that custom when
The Emperor of Monomotapa
Will drink. He takes his glass; the complete Court
At once set up prayers for him with a Voice

So loud, that all the neighbourhood aroused
Repeat the same, and on and on it sounds
Till the whole empire like a tempest swells
Its supplication for the monarch's tankard.

Such truths we owe to blest Geography,
That's certain as the magnet and the pole,
And by this learning we may scare aloof
All horned Chimaeras and vile Fallacies,
May know the world, and be the richest in it,
And keep the flag of Britain on the masts
Of thundering navies."

This great accent reached,
He paused, and nodded. The clock ticked, the fly
Walked round the Globe; till he, with sudden shock,
Struck with a silence, rubbed his eyes to find
The audience gone, plainly to view at once
Under his universal inspiration
Those fruitful wonders of the natural world.

JAPANESE GARLAND ❧

THE VISITOR

Suddenly the other side of this world wide,
Whose proud extent even conquering Steam allowed,
Grew near as the garden-gate; no mountain then,
No rosy-torturing desert, no dead lake,
Nor jungle, whirlpool, jealous frontier stopped us.
We moved within the wings of some ten words
Into a most familiar country air,
And like spring showers received it from the hills
That stood from our old hills ten thousand miles—
Or none; we paused along the yellow plains,
And kissed the child that ran from shyer friends
To take our hand; and we could tell what passed
In unknown language between old pouchy boat-men
Among the huge bullrushes where for ever
Dwells the uncaptured serpent six yards long,
Whom the small fish warping the waters' brim
Decline to notice. Then came orange-orchards,
Rising above the sea-cliff's bridle-roads;
And azure-flaming waves around rock-caves

Whence the pine thrust its elbows; then the dirge
Of sunless streams down cold black buttresses
Of vaster porticoes hurled up at heaven;
And then the patient mountain-stairs past peril,
Triumphant in the eyrie of a hamlet
That hears the constant silvering of the springs
And smiles in the mountain-steep among its cherries
Above the green air-crystal of the valley.
We knew them, we had seen the lights of evening
Moon-mimic here; and heard through dewbells dim
The strings that men cicada-like set murmuring.
Here, cried our hearts, tune might be found at length,
And all our dust laved in this garden of waters,
Our hurry halted by these giant rocks,
Whose coldness is a kindness, and above
There should be purer beams from heaven;

—no distance,

Sea, landslide, chasm, nor crossway of our life
Divided us that moment from the unknown
Pilgrimage singing in the stranger's mind.

ORNAMENTATIONS

The curving cranes with serpent necks
    Knotted on these enamelled streams,
The gloating mouths thrust out to vex
    The red-eyed war-gods' frenzy dreams,
The inscrutable and dog-like grin
Of demi-lions lock me in!

With countless crafty manacles
    Dead men's dexterity strives to bind,
Like some machine that all but feels,
    The amazed and apathizing mind.
Cornices, crannies, shape in shape,
Bud glittering eyes, defy escape.

Heavily hangs this haughty air,
    Drum, knell and drone commingling slow;
Claw-tendrils reach, man-monsters glare;
    The victim heart prepares to know
Art's terror, dragon genius—till
Thought spies one rose or daffodil.

FAR EAST

Old hamlets with your fragrant flowers
And honey for the bee,
Your curtained taverns, chiming towers,
Droning songs and twilight hours
And nodding industry—

Fine fields, wide-lapped, whose loveliest-born
Day's first bright cohort finds,
And steals away; whose lustier corn
The red-faced churl invades at morn
And proud as Caesar binds—

Uplands and groves that from the West
Have the last word for me,
Think not your image in my breast
Was darkened when I sang my best
Beside an Eastern sea.

Beside an Eastern sea the pines
In tufty spinneys drowse,
The firefly-grass beneath them shines

Blue-lanterned, and the chaliced vines
Climb witch-like to the boughs;

And girdled green there bask the plains
Where, with his timeless smiles,
And mushroom-hat, brown Vigour gains
His spindling roots, his haulms, his grains—
The Oriental Giles.

He serves a god much like your own,
Who, peeping from the rows,
Brings gourds the greatest ever grown,
And peerless pumpkins; smooths the down
Of these fruits, lacquers those.

Thence the young child at home awaits,
Bright-peering as a mouse,
Her share of country delicates,
And chatters bold to her young mates
About the smoky house.

The bronze cicada twangs all day,
And the silver-soft at night
Cools the snake's thicket by the way

Where heaps the sturdy disarray
Of husbandry's delights.

In rural music bold or frail
Contentment's anthem fills,
And, roving the rude-ripened vale,
If restless spirits sometime fail,
Here too are heavenly hills.

Sleep's master-dream there stands alone:
The mount of East and West!
The still hour come, his monstrous cone
Is a timid flower this morning blown,
Now folded like the rest.

EASTERN TEMPEST

That flying angel's torrent cry
Will hurl the mountains through the sky!
A wind like fifty winds at once
Through the bedragoned kingdom runs,
An army of rain slants icy stings
At many a wretch afield who clings
His cloak of straw, with glistening spines
Like a prodigious porcupine's.
The reptile grasses by his path
Wind sleek as unction from that Wrath
Which with a glassy claw uproots
The broad-leaved "kiri", flays and loots
Torn and snarled sinews, leaves for dead
The young crops with the shining head,
While blotched blunt melons darkly dot
The slaughtered swathes like cannon-shot.
The lotus in each pond upheaves
Its sacred, slow, appealing leaves,
And many a bush with wrestling jerk
Defies the daemon's murdeous work—
Yet nature stares white-lipped, to read
In Chance's eye what desperate deed?

A kinder god discerns, replies,
And stills the land's storm-shouts to sighs;
The clouds in massy folds apart
Disclose the day's bright bleeding heart,
Huge plumes and scarves black-tossing wide
As if a Kubla Khan had died!
From flame to flame the vision glows,
Till all the pools of heaven unclose
The lotus-light, the hue, the balm
Of wisdom infinitely calm.

INLAND SEA

Here in the moonlit sea,
While swift we fly, while tranced we gaze,
The fishers wind their ancient ways:
Now like sea-lilies loom their luring sails,
Or heaven's envoys walking fountained vales;
And now by one deflection dark,
Like waiting vultures of the night
Each pirate blackness skulks, a murderous mark
Begotten by a thing of light,
Like apprehension's baffling destiny.

THE QUICK AND THE DEAD

Once we three in Nara walked
Where pomp and fame look through the leaves;
With sabred shades we walked and talked
By lacquered gates and bow-like eaves,
By pools where carp doze through their green
Eternities, to lonelier shrines
Where mossy courtyards lie serene
Beneath some peasant-planted pines.

Less of that giant, surly bell
Whose black voice warned us at all hours
My late remembrance likes to tell,
Less of the Buddha as he lours
With thick curled skull and dead man's eye,
Of old wives' faithful groan of prayer,
Of fire-robed ritual trooping by,
Than the plain joy, three friends walked there.

THE INVIOLATE

There on the white Pacific shore the pines
Still serve their jealous gods, and late and soon
The murmur runs along their rugged lines,
"What black ship* waits the crash of our typhoon?"

And in this vigil circled, calm and proud,
God-gates temples glow with changeless noon,
Their mysteries luring that young seraph-cloud
Swan-like between the mountain and the moon.

**Black ship*, i.e. foreign warship, as introduced by Commodore Perry.

BUILDING THE LIBRARY TOKYO UNIVERSITY

Night Scene

Like men of fire, in painful night,
The Eastern builders thud
Their iron round; wild bubbles of light
From Babel's angles scud.

The hammer's fierce brain-battering shout
In bursts of power rebels,
Puts unheard melodies to rout,
Drowns heaven's songs and bells.

O swiftly serve their quiet will,
And build them one more home
Where nooks shall be most kind and still
For the great Muse to come!

ON A SMALL DOG

thrust out in a Tokyo street soon after his birth,
and rescued in vain

"Animula vagula blandula," foundling dear,
So deep a hold have you already won
On our tired hearts? So great a joy have you to
give?
So sharp a fear?
Can your tininess unseal so hot a tear
And prayer, that you should live?
Like these cherry-flowers here
Whose life thin-spun
Seems by its own ghost haunted—but no more
words!
Save, all heaven's luck befriend you,
Blind eyes and feeling hands,
That take us for all-surety and all-love,
And so to sleep.

THE AUTHOR'S LAST WORDS TO HIS STUDENTS*

Forgive what I, adventuring highest themes
Have spoiled and darkened, and the awkward hand
That longed to point the moral of man's dreams
And shut the wicket-gates of fairyland:
So by too harsh intrusion
Left colourless confusion.

For even the glories that I most revered,
Seen through my gloomed perspective in strange mood,
Were not what to our British seers appeared;
I spoke of peace, I made a solitude,
Herding with deathless graces
My hobbling commonplaces.

Forgive that eyeless lethargy which chilled
Your ardours and I fear dimmed much fine gold—
What your bright passion, leaping ages, thrilled

*In the school of English Literature, at the Tokyo Imperial University, 1924-1927.

To find and claim, and I yet dared withhold;
These and all chance offences
Against your finer senses.

And I will ever pray for your souls' health,
Remembering how, deep-tasked yet eager-eyed,
You loved imagination's commonwealth,
Following with smiling wonder a frail guide
Who hears beyond the ocean
The voice of your devotion.

MOODS, CONJECTURES AND FANCIES

FAMILIARITY

Dance not your spectral dance at me;
I know you well!
Along this lane there lives no tree
But I can tell.
I know each fall and rise and twist;
You—why, a wildflower in the mist,
The moon, the mist.

Sound not that long alarm, gray tower,
I know you well;
This is your habit at this hour,
You and your bell!
If once, I heard a hundred times
Through evening's ambuscade your chimes—
Dark tower, your chimes.

Enforce not that no-meaning so,
Familiar stream;
Whether you tune it high or low,
I know your theme;
A proud-fed but a puny rill,
A meadow brook, poured quick and shrill—
Alone and shrill.

Sprawl not so monster-like, blind mist;
    I know not "seems";
I am too old a realist
    To take sea-dreams
From you, or think a great white Whale
Floats through our hawthorn-scented vale—
    This foam-cold vale.

INACCESSIBILITY IN THE BATTLEFIELD

Forgotten streams, yet wishful to be known,
With humble moan
In rushy channels working, called us on;
These might have with as good result
Remained occult
And gray and dumb;
For where they curled and called we could
not come.

Some tottering hut they called the Moated Grange
Bade our steps range
And cramped routine for rural loves exchange;
That thatchéd spectre might as well
With some fierce shell
Have sunk to earth;
A jealous god declined our going forth.

And that delightful maybush, that above
The dead mill-drove
With rose-lipped courtesy and whispering love
Enchanted, was not ours to touch.

Between, this grutch,
This staring curse
Made a blind wall, and kept our lips averse.

The simple road proposed most kind desires
For further spires,
Hearths, garden-grots, dove-cots; but fang-fixed wires
And ambushed airy murder lay
All day, that way;
A simple road,—
The rampart where the fire-armed phantom strode.

WAR'S PEOPLE

Through the tender amaranthine domes
Of angel-evenings echoing summer song,
Through the black rock-tombs
Of winter, and where autumn floods prolong
The midnight roar and tumbling thunder,
Through spring's daisy-peeping wonder,
Round and beyond and over and under,
I see our homes.

Bloom, healing rosiness and wild-wine flowers,
Or lift a vain wing in the mire, dropt leaf;
Storm-spirit, coil your lightnings round mad towers;
Go forth, you marching Seasons, horsemen Hours;
Blow silver triumphs, Joy, and knell, grey Grief.

These after-pieces will not now dispel
The scene and action that was learned in hell.
These charming veils a thought has strength to waft
With one quick thrill aloft; and then we view

Seasons and hours we better knew,
Desperate budding of untimely green,
Skies and soft cloud-land savagely serene,
Steel or mere sleet that beat past-caring bones,
Night-tempest not so loud as those long moans
From low-gorged lairs, which outshine Zion's towers,
Weak rags of walls, the forts of godlike powers.
We went, returned,
But came with that far country learned;
Strange stars, and dream-like sounds, changed speech and law are ours.

DREAM ENCOUNTERS

The measureless houses of dreams,
And the magic of hours within hours;
And those who pass by like clear streams,
Pass by us, on a journey not ours!
The eyes that we know and we fear,
As waters of Castaly clear,
That gaze that once should have been sweet,
Now a terror to meet!
—Yet, both in one corridor narrowly led,
Those steps in another intensity tread;
There is space that convenes us, but holds us apart;
Sunlight and sunlight, distinctly combined,
As a wish with the wind
And all heaven with one heart.

PARABLE

Wide as the world is, music abounds,
Time has a legion of lovely sounds
From the soonest blackbird to latest bee
That murmurs along his honeying rounds;
 Surpassing those, one anthem is sweet
 As ever the message of Paraclete,
 When the kiss of Spring
 Says all must sing
 And the host of secrets are bright on the wing.
Then the willow, that last in the moon stood numb,
Finds its Apollo-vesture come,
And, waiting on zephyr-sense so long,
Communes its sudden vein of song
Till on to the white and blue serene
One willow sings from a hamlet green.

Long are the sighs that lull the sleep
Of breathing youngness in such new hours.
Breezes are come to dance the flowers
But from what deep,

What siren shores!
Such nights, the moon's still self can stir
The feathery spray of this one tree,
And allure the least to tune with her—
She sways these leaves that sways the sea.
And far I hear the answer given;
Responding triumph will not pause,
Dares trespass the ethereal laws.
The ploughman's mark, the hatchet's toy,
Magicked into a wingéd Joy,
Reveals new song to Heaven.

A SUNRISE IN MARCH

While on my cheek the sour and savage
wind
Confuses soul with sense, while unamazed
I view the siege of pale-starred horror raised
By dawn whose waves charge stern and crimson-
lined,
In cold blue tufts of battle-smoke afar,
And sable crouching thickets by my way—
While I thus droop, the living land grows gay
With starry welcomes to the conquering star!

From every look-out whence they watch him win
(That angry Cromwell!) high on thorn and bine
The selfless wildbirds hail their holy light:
With changes free as flute or violin,
To naked fields they peal as proud and fine
As though they had not dreamed of death all
night.

FRAGMENT

Steal abroad, your time is come; doubt not
once the new-blown hour;
Winter's wickedness is past,
And those long leaden nerveless moods
Which frowned much worse than frozen
woods
Gone, as soft as thistle-wool
Upon a zephyr's love-like breath;
In animation beautiful
Returns your chance; now wander with
The sparkle on the living seas,
Nor fear that in these green estates
Ambushed may lie
The hooded serpent with the human eye;
But all is opening garden-gates,
Running mill-sails, fountain trees,
Winged boats that water-jewels attend
Where singingly they round the bend;
And sounding works whose smoke lifts
proud
Through towers of force to yon rose-cloud

From elemental engines poured—
And both a glory to the Lord.
From mill to steeple, day breaks pure;
Your horse is on the road he wished,
And away past suburb and colure
Goes like the famous giant refreshed;
While you as light you travel by
See beckoning hand or smiling eye
That came in night's dark fairy showers
To make new morning wild with flowers

* * *

SUMMER RAINSTORM

Sweet conversations, woodland incantations
Are thrilling through the tides of gale and shower,
Which now conceal,
Now blue-reveal,
Across the fallow's russet undulations
A broken windmill and a silent tower.

And sometimes glancing through the top sprigs dancing
Elf-wings set out on visit and patrol.
Though the full cloud
Frowns monster-browed,
Those merry wild-folk chirruping and chancing
Know the kind truth; would I had such a soul!

Joy's masque and fashion of Time's Samson-passion
Deceives no lark that springs from weed and clod.
Through their frank sight
I feel the bright
Angel-event of sunset's fresh creation
And fields made lovely with the living God.

THE KILN

Beside the creek where seldom oar or sail
Adventures, and the gulls whistling like
Patrol the pasture of the falling tide, [men
Like Timon's mansion stands the silent kiln.
Half citadel, half temple, strong it stands
With layered stones built into cavernous curves,
The fire-vault now as cool as leaves and stones
And dews can be. Here came my flitting thought,
The only visitor of a sunny day,
Except the half-mad wasp that fights with all,
The leaping cricket in his apple-green,
And emerald beetle with his golden helmet;
While the south wind woke all the colony
Of sorrels and sparse daisies, berried ivies
And thorns bowed down with sloes, and brambles
Offering a feast that no child came to take. [red

In these unwanted derelicts of man
Nature has touched the picture with a smile
Of more than usual mystery; the far heights
With thunderous forest marshalled are her toil,
But this her toy, her petty larceny

That pleased her, lurking like a gipsy girl,
My thought came here with artfulness like hers
To spy on her, and, though she fled, pursued
To where on eastern islands, in the cells
Of once grave seers, her iris woos the wind.

THE CORRELATION

Again that yellow dusk or light along
The winter hills: again the trees' black claws
Waiting and working by the bridge of space:
Again the tower, among tombs a huge tomb;
White scattered birds, a black horse in the meads,
And the eel-track of the brown stream fringing by.

Would understanding win herself my vote,
Now, having known this crisis thirty years,
She should decide me why it overwhelms
My chart of time and history; should declare
What in the spirit of a man long schooled
To human concept and devotion dear,
Upraised by sure example, undefiled
By misery and defeat, still in the sun—
What stirs in him, and finds its brother-self,
From that late sky. Again that sky, that tower,
These effigies and wizardries of chance,
Those soundless vollies of pale and distant birds
Have taken him, and from his whirring toils
Made him as far away, as unconcerned,
As consonant with the Power as its bare trees.

AUTUMN IN THE WEALD

Come, for here the lazy night
With rosy camp-fires blossoms bright,
The stream half-runs with flute-like trill
Through the quaint channels of the mill
And, to accentuate the hush,
Through fine bamboo and needled rush
A water-spirit ferries. Come,
And see how kindly all's at home.
No sweeter things than these I rhyme,
And this by much their sweetest time.
Then, sweet, agree, and by this gate
Watch each one gathering to his mate,
To nest or warren, bough or byre—
The dearness answers all desire,
When all, the shepherd, dog and sheep
With sleep-like motions welcome sleep;
The elm-tree's momentary stir
And freshened sluices yield to her,
And though the fire-side shout and song
Defy her there, they will not long.

The bonfire's crackling zeal dies down,

The laughing supper-groups are gone,
The fair falls quiet in Yalding town,
Alone with the mist I linger on.

RETURN

Deed and event of prouder stature
    Dare not always overshade
The first fresh buddings of our nature;
    Their hidden colour does not fade.

We well may quit our laboured action
    At some sweet call to early loves,
And find the jewel of self-contraction
    Like saints in rocks and springs and groves.

Win back the world when true Aurora
    Dawned a goddess, not an hour!
Think, have you caught the smile of Flora
    Since your own life was a young flower?

And Love, even Love, has dropped her lilies
    On the hot highroad; once she knew
How columbines and daffadillies
    Created her own sun and dew.

Return; how stands that man enchanted
    Who, after seas and mountains crossed,
Finds his old threshold, so long scanted,
    With not a rose or robin lost!

The wise, from passion now retreating
To the hamlets of the mind,
In every glance have claimed the greeting
Of spirits infinitely kind.

THE DEEPER FRIENDSHIP

Were all eyes changed, were even poetry cold,
Were those long systems of hope that I tried to deploy
Skeletons, still I should keep one final hold,
Since clearer and clearer returns my first-found joy.

I would go, once more, through the sunless autumn in trouble;
Thin and cold rain dripping down through branches black,
Streams hoarse-hurrying and pools spreading over the stubble,
And the waggoner leaving the hovel under his sack

Would guide me along by the gate and deserted siding,
The inn with the tattered arbour, the choking weir;
And yet, security there would need small guiding.

I know one hearth, one love that shine beyond
  fear.

There, though the sharpest storm and flood were
  abroad,
And the last husk and leaf were stripped from
  the tree,
I would sue for peace where the rats and mice
  have gnawed,
And well content that Nature should bury me.

THE BLIND LEAD THE BLIND

Dim stars like snowflakes are fluttering in
heaven,
Down the cloud-mountains by wind-torrents
riven;
There are still chances, but one more than all
Slowly burns out on the sea's dark wall—
The best ever given.

One, the divinest, goes down to the dark,
In a red sullen vanishing, a poor stifled spark.
You, who have reason, were staring at this
As though by your gaze it would clear the abyss—
It was once your sea-mark.

Hear on the shore too the sighed monotones
Of waves that in weakness slip past the purled
stones;
The seethe of blown sand round the dry fractured
hull,
Salt-reeds and tusked fence; hear the struck gull
With death in his bones.

Slow comes the net in, that's filled with frustra-
tion;

Night ends the day of thwart discreation;
I would be your miracle-worker, sad friend,
Bid a music for you and a new star ascend,—
    But I know isolation.

REPORT ON EXPERIENCE

I have been young, and now am not too old;
And I have seen the righteous forsaken,
His health, his honour and his quality taken.
This is not what we were formerly told.

I have seen a green country, useful to the race,
Knocked silly with guns and mines, its villages vanished,
Even the last rat and last kestrel banished—
God bless us all, this was peculiar grace.

I knew Seraphina; Nature gave her hue,
Glance, sympathy, note, like one from Eden.
I saw her smile warp, heard her lyric deaden;
She turned to harlotry;—this I took to be new.

Say what you will, our God sees how they run.
These disillusions are His curious proving
That He loves humanity and will go on loving;
Over there are faith, life, virtue in the sun.

EPITAPH

Happily through my years this small stream ran;
It charmed the boy, and purified the man;
Its hollowed banks were my romantic caves,
Its winter tumults made my ocean waves.
I had no gold, nor silver overmuch,
But what its sunny falls disclosed as such,
And wished no gem, when eyes could here be bright
With the kingfisher's sapphire beam of flight,
Or the pearl shield that tilting fish below
Through arras of blue water-mosses show.
What need for templed lotus, when our stream
Enthroned the yellow lily? there the dream
Of placid Buddha might be as secure;
Visitant wings there were that loved the lure.

With all my years this pretty stream sang on.
I brought one here to praise it; who is gone,
Yet in that crystal soul her mirrored face
With foxgloves looking in still finds a place.
Even the Muse's "melody unheard"

For me is woven with this water's word,
Since here I sat to read immortal song;
The ripple played to that, nor answered wrong.
All that deep-sighing elegy might mourn,
Glad lyric hail, and sonnet-thought adorn,
The changeful rivulet from stone to stone
Enchanted into anthems of its own.

My travel then! my wealth, my dream, my love,
True Golden Treasury and Golden Grove!
Accept one weakness, let one pale shade cling
Where with so strong a life you run and sing.

ON A BIOGRAPHICAL DICTIONARY

Proud is assembly, and the anthem proud
That populous nave and aisle and gallery raise
In conscious strength, till God in his bright cloud
Seems hovering to that multitude of praise.
Yet from this mild prosaic book, as loud,
As strong, as various, from as many throats,
I hear the Gloria of a golden crowd,
And there the heavenly wing still brighter floats.

I hear the trumpet and alarm of time
Appeal, and men and women of great soul
Replying, singing to their genius climb;
Deep wisdoms hearten, organ-yearnings roll;
Tried faith transfigures every imperfection
Into one chant, one radiance and election.

A QUARTET

("The Mikado" at Cambridge)

Four singers with a Delphic seriousness
In harmony's kind problem play their part,
And I, who see and hear, think they express
Nature's best gift, the calm delight of art.
The fourfold music takes its twining ways,
And like a rich spring underwood embowers
Their careful theme, which from the tonal maze
Sudden as a nightingale all bright out-flowers
When that dark lady bids a madrigal.
O sweet content, reward in deed, release
Of spirit here in imperfection shut;
Symmetry's answer given without a "but";
Deep-moved I mark their choral masterpiece,
Their union in each swell and dying fall.

A CONNOISSEUR

Presume not that gray idol with the scythe
  And hourglass of the stern perpetual sands
To be a mere insensate mill of hours,
Unawed by battles, unbeguiled with flowers;
Think, this old Merlin may be vexed or blithe,
And for the future stretches hungry hands.

No last year's bride discovers more caprice
Than this bald magpie smuggling up his wit,
And in his crumbling belfry, where the cost
Of high-born death in plundered ruin's lost,
Nodding his glory to each glittering piece
Of glass or jewel that his fancy hit.

Close in the shop of some lean artizan,
Who carves a snuff-box for Squire Harkaway,
Time stoops, and stares, and knows his destined
  prize:
Croesus shall hunt this modest merchandise
When frieze and pillar of a master's plan
Are crushed in waggon-tracks to bind the clay.

There stalled theology makes angels weep

In twenty volumes blazoned red and gold,
And there a broadside's bawled about the street;
Time fetched his halfpence out and bought a
sheet.
The twenty volumes slumber in a heap,
The ballad among heirlooms lives enrolled.

Lordly oration thronged the sculptured roof,
And pamphleteered in plaudits through the town;
The charlatan proclaimed his draughts and pills,
And tossed the crowd his woodcuts and his bills;
From rhetoric's remains Time flies aloof,
And hears the quack still pattering to the clown.

Voluptuous canvas! Venus in May-bloom,
Sunshine of vital gold, faun-twinkling groves,
Harmonious limbs and volant veils, go mourn;
For you will lie with fire, while Time has borne
The blue-daubed frigate from the servants' room
To swell the mad collection of his loves.

SIR WILLIAM TRELOAR'S DINNER FOR CRIPPLED CHILDREN

This is an ancient England in the new;
Hear how those thousand children leap and sing.
Their dreams, their wonder and their pleasure ring
Through England; young expectancy comes true,
While Mayor and Alderman and Usher bright
With robes and jewels out of a fairy story,
And brighter hearts, wish them their heart's delight,
And music shows them sudden streets of glory.

Here walks the shade of Whittington in bliss;
O greatness and good-nature, still you thrive.
I thank my God, Charles Lamb is still alive
In these new Londoners; they shall not miss
The crown of life; here's Coram, Dickens, Hood,
Christmas and Christ profoundly understood.

THE STUDY

While I sit penning plans of dead affairs,
And hardly pause but when some wilder gust
Drives the mist shower with a more savage thrust
Against my window, hark! what sweeter cares
Find a shy voice, that makes my writing cease,
And in this room of shelves, and books, and files,
The ranked and crested past, what pleasure smiles!
The dead withdraw, the living shares their peace.

For down my chimney with the dripping rain
Come tiny trills and chirps and silvery notes
Like whistling mice; it's nesting-time again;
There in the dimness gape what eager throats
Of the new brood, who through this tempest dun
Know they are for the singing and the sun!

VALUES

Till darkness lays a hand on these gray eyes
  And out of man my ghost is sent alone,
It is my chance to know that force and size
Are nothing but by answered undertone.
No beauty even of absolute perfection
Dominates here—the glance, the pause, the guess
Must be my amulets of resurrection;
Raindrops may murder, lightnings may caress.

There I was tortured, but I cannot grieve;
There crowned and palaced—visibles deceive.
That storm of belfried cities in my mind
Leaves me my vespers cool and eglantined.
From love's wide-flowering mountain-side I chose
This sprig of green, in which an angel shows.

¶ Hand-set in Deepdene type by Elaine & Arthur Rushmore at the Golden Hind Press in Madison, New Jersey. One hundred and five copies have been printed on special mould-made paper from Holland and signed by the author. Harper & Brothers, Publishers, New York and London. Anno Domini MDCCCCXXX